# A Note to Parents and Teachers

SAINSBURY'S READING SCHEME is a compelling new reading programme for children, designed in conjunction with leading literacy experts, including Cliff Moon M.Ed., Honorary Fellow of the University of Reading. Cliff Moon has spent many years as a teacher and teacher educator specializing in reading and has written more than 140 books for children and teachers. He reviews regularly for teachers' journals.

Beautiful illustrations and superb full-colour photographs combine with engaging, easy-to-read stories to offer a fresh approach to each subject. Each book in the SAINSBURY'S READING SCHEME programme is guaranteed to capture a child's interest while developing his or her reading skills, general knowledge, and love of reading.

The five levels of the programme are aimed at different reading abilities, enabling you to choose the books that are exactly right for your child:

**Yellow Level** – Learning to read
**Green Level** – Beginning to read
**Gold Level** – Beginning to read alone
**Ruby Level** – Reading alone
**Sapphire Level** – Proficient readers

The "normal" age at which a child begins to read can be anywhere from three to eight years old, so these levels are only a general guideline.

No matter which level you select, you can be sure that you are helping your child learn to read, then read to learn!

LONDON, NEW YORK, MUNICH,
MELBOURNE, AND DELHI

**Project Editor** Shaila Awan
**Art Editor** Susan Calver
**Senior Editor** Linda Esposito
**Senior Managing Art Editor** Peter Bailey
**US Editor** Regina Kahney
**Production** Kate Oliver
**Picture Researcher** Martin Redfern
**Jacket Designer** David McDonald
**Natural History Consultant**
Theresa Greenaway

**Reading Consultant**
Linda B. Gambrell, Ph.D.

This edition published in 2011
First published in Great Britain in 1998 by
Dorling Kindersley Limited,
80 Strand, London WC2R 0RL
Penguin Group (UK)

A CIP record for this book is available from the British Library.

ISBN 978-1-4053-7563-4

Colour reproduction by Colourscan, Singapore
Printed and bound in China by L. Rex Printing Co. Ltd.

The publisher would like to thank the following for their kind
permission to reproduce their photographs:
Key: t=top, b=below, l=left, r=right, c=center

**Biofotos:** C. Andrew Henley 14–15; **Bruce Coleman:** Gerald Cubitt
24br; M.P.L. Fogden 9bl; Peter Zabransky 17tr; **FLPA:** Larry West
23br; **NHPA:** Stephen Dalton 12–13, 27tr; OSF: G.I. Bernard 29br; J.A.L.
Cooke 15tr; **Planet Earth Pictures:** Brian Kenney 26–27; **Warren
Photographic:** Kim Taylor 13cr.

**Additional photography by** Jane Burton, Neil Fletcher, Frank
Greenaway, Colin Keates, Harry Taylor, Kim Taylor, Jerry Young

All other images © Dorling Kindersley.
For further information see www.dkimages.com

Discover more at
# www.dk.com

Sainsbury's
Reading Scheme

Gold Level
**Beginning to read alone**

# Bugs! Bugs! Bugs!

Written by Jennifer Dussling

DK

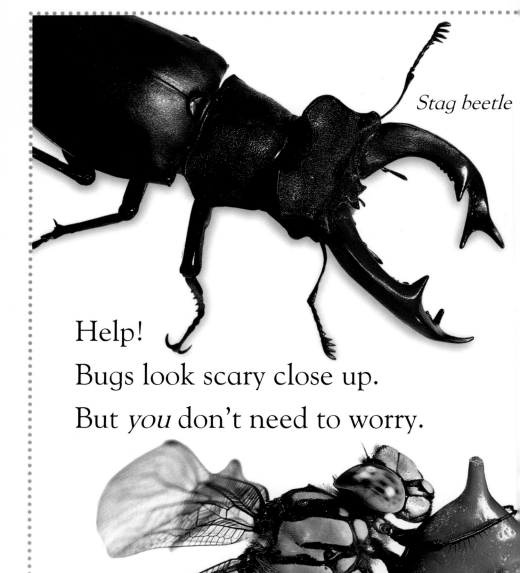

*Stag beetle*

Help!
Bugs look scary close up.
But *you* don't need to worry.

*Dragonfly*

Most bugs are a danger
only to other insects.
They are the bugs
that really bug
other bugs.

*Praying
mantis*

*Weevil-
hunting
wasp*

This praying mantis
sits perfectly still.
But if you are a bug,
watch out!
A fly lands on a branch
near a praying mantis.
The mantis fixes
its big eyes on the fly.

In a second,
the mantis lashes out.
Its long front legs trap the fly.
The mantis pulls the fly
into its mouth.
Munch, crunch –
soon the fly is gone!

Some bugs hunt other bugs,
not to eat themselves,
but to feed to their babies.
This hunting wasp
has just stung a weevil.

*Weevil-hunting wasp*

It will drag the weevil to its nest and
lay eggs on the weevil.
When the eggs hatch,
the young wasps, called grubs,
will eat up the weevil.

## Hairy food

The spider-hunting
wasp catches huge
spiders for its grubs.
Sometimes it takes over
the spider's home, too!

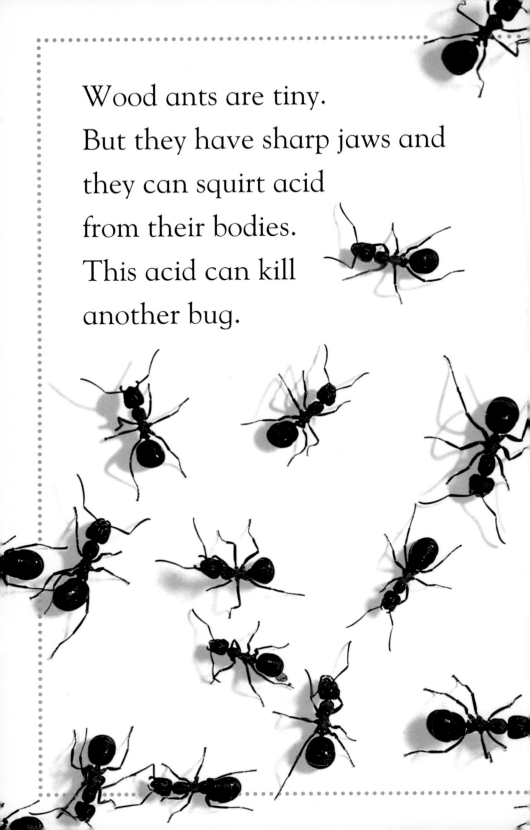

Wood ants are tiny.
But they have sharp jaws and
they can squirt acid
from their bodies.
This acid can kill
another bug.

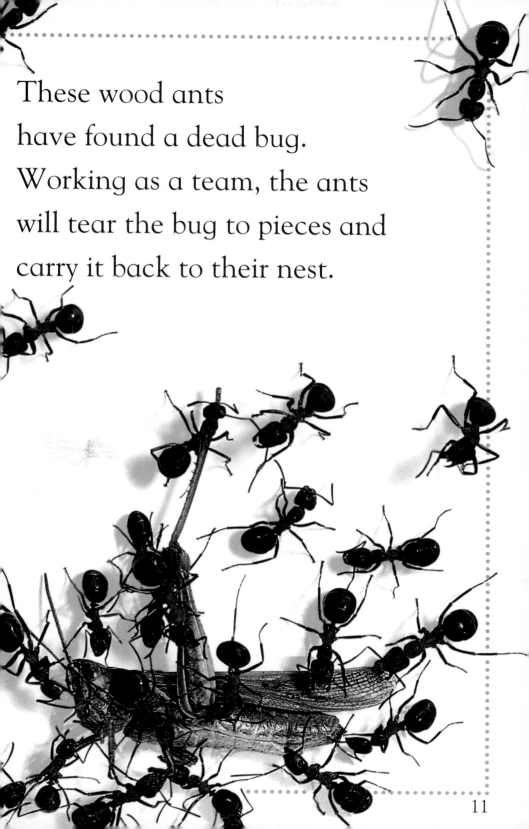

These wood ants
have found a dead bug.
Working as a team, the ants
will tear the bug to pieces and
carry it back to their nest.

It's a quiet day by a pond.
One second, a mosquito
is buzzing along.
The next second,
a dragonfly swoops down and
snaps the mosquito
right out of the air!

Dragonflies are flying killers
that eat and eat and eat.
In half an hour, they can eat
their own body weight.
That's like you eating
250 sandwiches!

**Ancient insect**
Dragonflies were around
long before the dinosaurs!
This dragonfly rotted away
millions of years ago.
It left its print in a rock.

An assassin is a person who kills
another person on purpose.
The assassin bug is a bug
that really lives up
to its name.

**Kissing bugs**

Some assassin bugs
are called kissing bugs.
This is because
they often bite people
on the face.

When it catches another insect,
it injects the insect with poison.

The poison turns
the bug's insides to soup.
Then the assassin bug
sucks up the soup!

Only one bug
has to watch out for
a male stag beetle –
another male stag beetle!
What do they fight about?
Usually a female
stag beetle!

**Short, sharp jaws**
A female stag beetle
has smaller jaws
than a male.
But she can give
a much sharper bite.

The fighting beetles
poke at each other,
then lock jaws.

One beetle grabs
the other beetle
and throws him.
The loser
scurries away.

*Monarch
butterfly
caterpillar*

With so many killer bugs and
other hungry animals,
how do any insects survive?

*Hoverfly*

*Click beetle*

All these bugs have special ways
to trick their enemies.
You can read about them
if you turn the page.

*Postman
butterfly
caterpillar*

Stinkbugs have glands
that make smells.
Some stinkbugs
ooze a nasty-smelling liquid
when they are in danger.
That's a big turn-off!

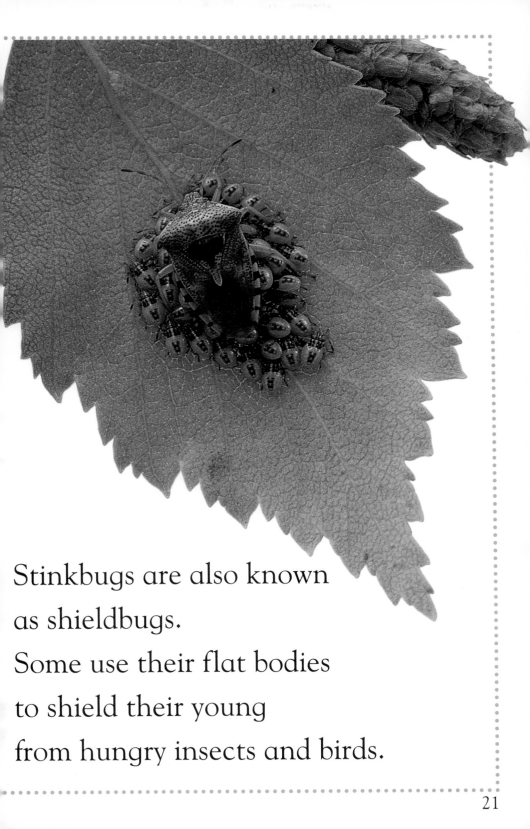

Stinkbugs are also known
as shieldbugs.
Some use their flat bodies
to shield their young
from hungry insects and birds.

The monarch butterfly
looks easy to capture and eat.
But hungry bugs and birds
leave it alone.
Why?

In the insect world,
bright colours are a warning.
Bright orange signals that
this butterfly tastes bad.
The monarch butterfly caterpillars
taste awful too!

**Changing faces**
When a caterpillar
is fully grown,
it changes into a butterfly
inside a hard case like this,
called a chrysalis (KRISS-uh-liss).

*Tropical lappet moth caterpillar*

This caterpillar has long hairs that break easily.
When enemies try to catch it, they get a mouthful of hair instead!

**Safety in numbers**
Caterpillars sometimes huddle together.
They flick their heads up to startle a hungry enemy.

And this spiky caterpillar
can be deadly.
The leaves that it eats
make its body poisonous.
It is not harmed by the poison but
its enemies are!

*Postman
butterfly
caterpillar*

A thornbug is good at hiding.
It looks like a thorn on a twig.
A bird looking for a meal
might not see it.

Thornbugs are clever, too.
Sometimes they all face
the same way and
stay very still!

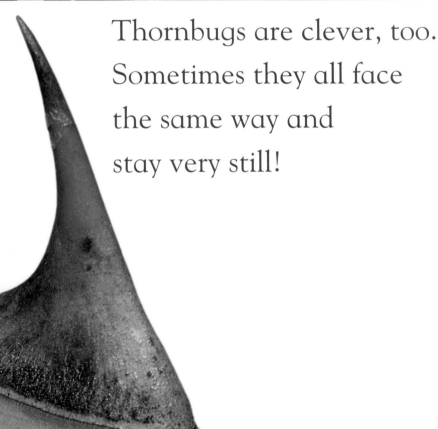

To avoid being eaten,
this click beetle
has a clever way of escaping.

It arches its back and then
jumps into the air.

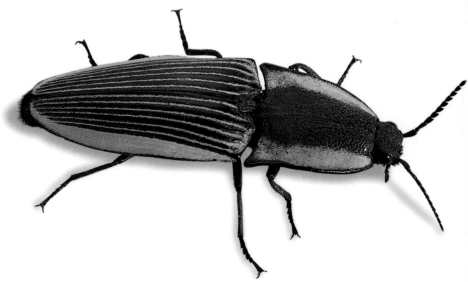

If the beetle
lands upside down,
it throws itself into the air again –
this time hoping to land safely
on its feet!

## Flashing lights

Some click beetles
send out light signals.
These flashing lights
help the beetles
to find a mate.

One of these bugs
is a harmless hoverfly.
The other is a hornet
with a nasty sting.
Can you tell
which is which?
No?

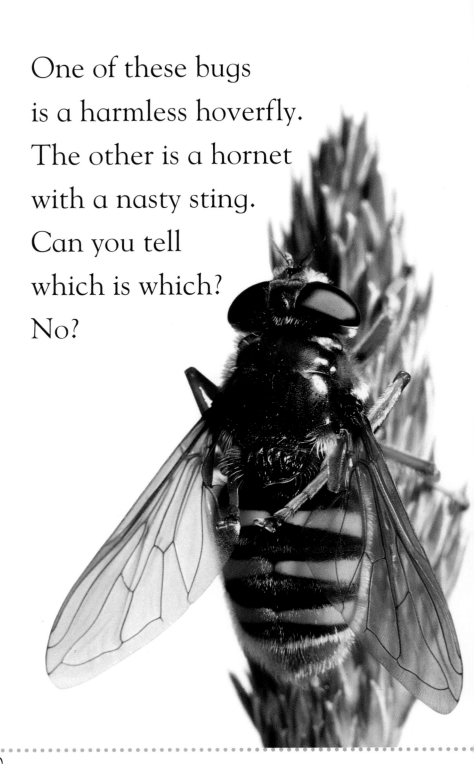

Neither can most bugs and birds!
That's why they leave
both of these insects alone.
Do you still not know which is which?
The fly is the bug
on the left!

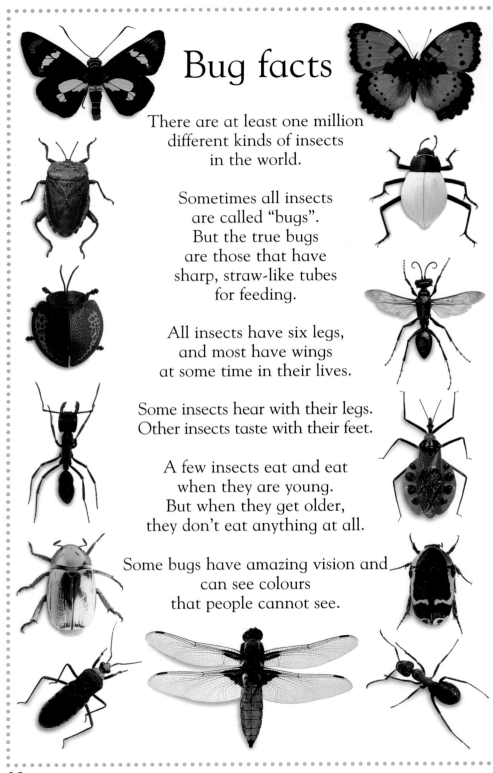

# Bug facts

There are at least one million
different kinds of insects
in the world.

Sometimes all insects
are called "bugs".
But the true bugs
are those that have
sharp, straw-like tubes
for feeding.

All insects have six legs,
and most have wings
at some time in their lives.

Some insects hear with their legs.
Other insects taste with their feet.

A few insects eat and eat
when they are young.
But when they get older,
they don't eat anything at all.

Some bugs have amazing vision and
can see colours
that people cannot see.

**Sainsbury's**
Reading Scheme

# CERTIFICATE
## of READING

My name is

_____

I have read

_____

Date

_____